NOV

7

the new aga cook

No.2 cooking for kids

Also in the series

Breakfast & Brunch

Good Food Fast

Laura James

the new aga cook

No 2 cooking for kids

Absolute Press

the new aga cook

First published in 2003

First published in the United Kingdom by
Absolute Press
Scarborough House, 29 James Street West, Bath, England BA1 IAS.
Tel: 44 (0) 1225 316013
Fax: 44 (0) 1225 445836
E-mail: office@absolutepress.co.uk
Website: www.absolutepress.co.uk

ISBN 1 904573 06 1

Photography: Andy Davis
Food styling: Penny Chambers

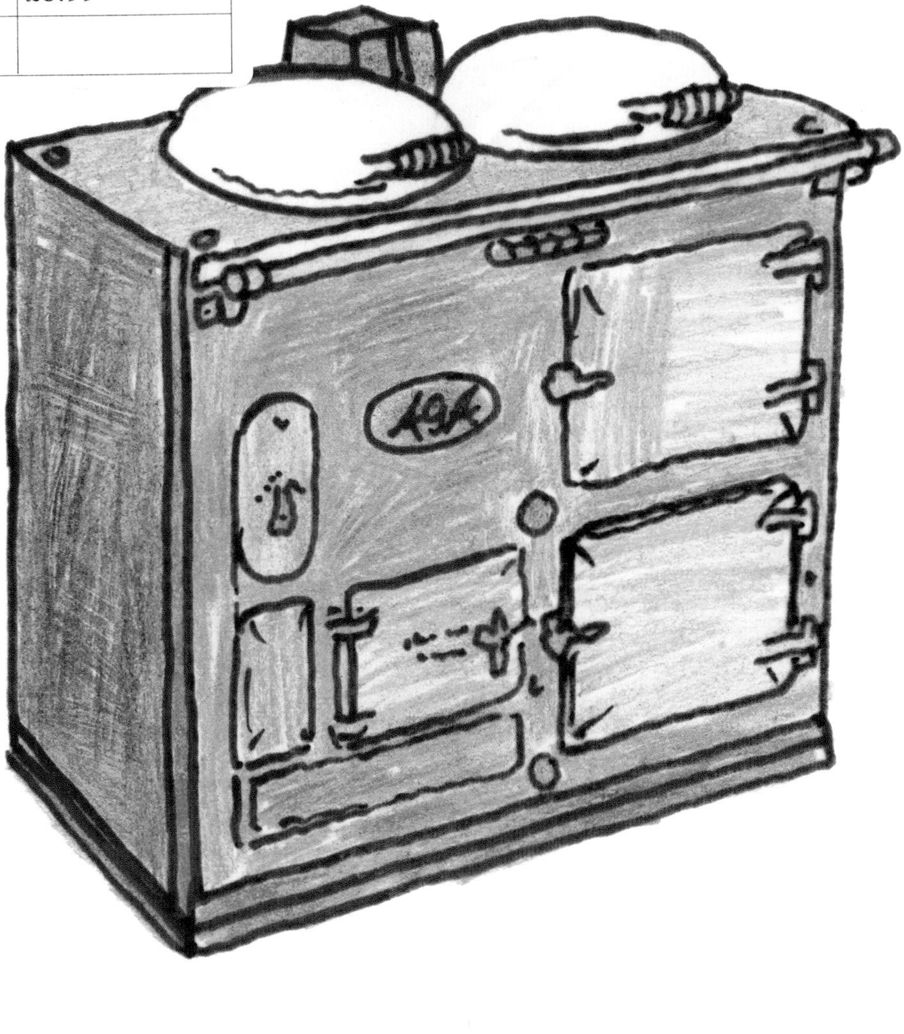

For Jack and Toby

Who make life – and cooking – a joy

cooking for kids
menu

Something as simple as licking a spoonful

intro

There are few things in the world as lovely as a few hours spent in the kitchen with children. Forget shopping for wildly expensive shoes or being pampered to within an inch of your life. A lovely happy child covered in flour and chattering away while enjoying one of life's most basic pleasures is, for me at least, time sent from heaven.

Don't you find when cooking with children that you often end up creating far more than a batch of biscuits? The kitchen is often the place where you'll hear about the things that are really close to a child's heart.

Whether it's first-time finger-painting or a new boyfriend, for some reason they're more likely to tell you about it if they're up to their elbows in dough.

I believe the most important thing about entertaining children in the kitchen is to make it fun. They spend so much time engaged in high-tech pursuits that something as simple as licking a spoonful of deliciously gooey cake mixture can seem to them so marvellous. The recipes in this book are things we eat all the time. They're also recipes that I've cooked with all my children. Many of them make a quick weekday supper or after-school snack.

Sometimes when I'm cooking I can't move for children wanting to help, while at other times they'd far rather get on with something else and leave the work

of cake mixture can seem so marvellous

to me. Whatever their mood, I love having them in the kitchen with me – learning to cook and becoming familiar with food is one of life's most basic skills and best learned in the kitchen at home.

An Aga kitchen is the heart of the home, a place where memories are made. There are few things a parent remembers as tear-jerkingly vividly as their child proudly showing off something they've made themselves or hearing that wonderful phrase "my mummy makes the best..."

I believe no child should enter their teenage years without having made at least one batch of fairy cakes or having subjected his parents to a truly hideous meal that he's made "especially for them".

I'm a realist when it comes to children and food, firmly believing that they shouldn't be 'tricked' into eating things they don't like by disguising hated food as something else.

All you can do, I think, is try to encourage a healthy relationship with food and make cooking and eating as much fun as it can be.

So enjoy cooking with your children. Involve them and indulge them and I guarantee you'll have delicious fun...

Laura James

Whatever their mood, I love having children

in the kitchen with me. It's delicious fun

after-school treats

Children can arrive home from school hungry and fractious. It doesn't always work out so, but to prevent a raid on the pantry I try to give mine quick, nutritious snacks to keep them going until supper. Sometimes I'll rustle up something they can help with, but often I'll sit them at the kitchen table with a pile of crayons and some paper and prepare something while they draw…

My youngest son would only get on the Eurostar

croque monsieur

Quick and easy – the problem is avoiding eating it before it makes it on to your child's plate. If your children don't like ham, you can simply substitute tomatoes

1 egg
Splash of full-fat milk
Freshly ground black pepper
A little soft butter
4 thick slices of bread
2 slices of ham
2 slices of Emmental

In a shallow bowl, beat the egg, adding a little milk and pepper. Butter the bread on one side. Put the ham and cheese between the bread on the buttered side and press each made-up sandwich into the eggy mixture in the bowl.

Heat a cast-iron frying pan on the simmering plate for a couple of minutes. Place each sandwich in the pan.

Cook for a couple of minutes until the underneath is a gorgeous golden colour and the cheese has started to melt.

Flip the sandwich over in the pan and cook the other side for a couple of minutes.

Take the sandwich out of the pan and cut it into quarters. Then serve and watch it disappear!

Serves 2 – but they won't stop at that!

once he was told this dish originated in France

aga cheese on toast

There's something about this ridiculously simple dish cooked in an Aga that makes it taste absolutely blissful. It's the perfect tea-time treat for children – it takes minutes and is packed full of protein

1 slice of Cheddar cheese
1 slice of Red Leicester
2 slices of white bread
1 slice of streaky bacon

If you were to butter the bread before putting on the cheese, this recipe would be a version of Scotch Rabbit, slightly more child-friendly than its Welsh counterpart. I absolutely refuse to call it 'rarebit', since I firmly believe that name was conjured up by people who feel the need to make language more complicated than it should be. The fact is that since the early 18th century cooks have been writing about Welsh Rabbit, so that's how it should stay!

There's something about the way the bacon melts into the cheese that gives it a deliciously salty taste.

Cut the cheese into inch-wide (2.5cm) strips and place on the bread, alternating the cheeses so you end up with stripes. Cut the bacon into little pieces and sprinkle on top.

Cook on a baking sheet on the floor of the roasting oven for about six minutes. The bread will toast underneath, so there's no need to toast it first.

Serve with a crisp green salad and, if you like them, some plain potato crisps.

Serves 1

A firm favourite that disappears at great speed!

simple banana bread

A true taste of childhood and wonderful warm or cold, banana bread is so delicious that it disappears almost as soon as it's baked. Spread it with lashings of unsalted butter and wait for the rush

125g (4 ¹/₂ oz) of soft butter
125g (4 ¹/₂ oz) of golden caster sugar
2 eggs
1 teaspoon of vanilla extract
4 large bananas
175g (6 oz) of plain flour
Pinch of salt
¹/₂ teaspoon of bicarbonate of soda
2 teaspoons of baking powder
3 tablespoons of full-fat milk
900g (2 lb) loaf tin

Having children who are almost pathologically afraid of 'bits', my banana bread contains no sultanas, raisins or nuts, although you should feel free to add them if you want to.

Mix the butter and sugar together in a bowl. Add the eggs and vanilla extract and continue mixing until smooth. Mash the bananas and add them to the mix. Then slowly add the flour, salt, bicarbonate of soda, milk and baking powder. Grease and line a loaf tin and pour in the mixture. For a two-oven Aga, put the grid shelf on the floor of the roasting oven with the cold, plain shelf on the second set of runners. For a three-oven or four-oven Aga, put the grid shelf on the lowest set of runners in the baking oven and slide in the tin. Bake for about 45 minutes.

Makes one loaf

It's lovely warm and spread thickly with butter

chocolate and banana toastie

Banana and chocolate is a perfect combination. Remember those chocolate-coated banana sweets sold alongside lurid pink shrimps and sugar mice with string tails? This is the sandwich equivalent

1 ripe banana
1 teaspoon of full-fat milk
Healthy dollop of Green & Black's
**   chocolate spread**
Butter for spreading
4 slices of thick white bread

For years I had an aversion to banana sandwiches, remembering – with a shudder – soggy offerings packed in Tupperware and reluctantly eaten at the back of the school bus.

However, my youngest son has always adored bananas (and chocolate come to that), and this sandwich came about as a way to persuade him to eat something he could pick up himself when he was tiny.

In a bowl, mash the banana with the milk. Spread one side of each slice of the bread with a little butter and then the chocolate spread. Then spread the banana mixture on one side and make into sandwiches.

Put the sandwiches in the Aga toaster and place them on the simmering plate, with the lid down, for a couple of minutes on each side.

Makes two sandwiches

Grab the children, take the phone off the hook

classic tuna melt

This classic couldn't be simpler. Served with a salad, it makes

a quick and easy supper for those days when you're frantic.

You can, of course, use any bread you happen to have around

Small tin of tuna
1 tablespoon of mayonnaise
2 slices of ciabatta
2 thin slices of Gruyère

Most children like tuna. It's good for them and a perfect store cupboard basic, making the Tuna Melt a real winner. You can do all sorts of things to spice it up, including adding a splash of Worcestershire sauce, a couple of anchovies or even some fried onions.

Mix the tuna and mayonnaise together. Spread on the ciabatta. Top with the cheese and place on a baking sheet. Put the baking sheet on the floor of the roasting oven and cook for a few minutes. Then move it to the top of the roasting oven and cook until the cheese starts to bubble.

Serve with a crisp green salad.

Makes enough for one

and eat these up while no one's looking!

ice cream parlour milk shake

My daughters, Lucie and Tatti, invented this drink while messing around in the kitchen one day. It was the result of a tussle over a packet of Maltesers and it tastes almost too scrummy

1 scoop of vanilla ice cream
$1/_2$ pint (10 fl oz) of full-fat milk
1 packet of Maltesers
1 banana
1 tablespoon of chocolate syrup
4 mini marshmallows

When Whiteleys in Bayswater was newly opened and my eldest daughter was very small, I used to sneak off there and hang out in the ice cream parlour drinking chocolate malts, with her babbling away to herself in her pram.

From that moment on she was a bit of a milk shake fiend and still adores them to this day.

Chop the bananas into small pieces and place them, along with everything else except the marshmallows and Maltesers, into the blender.

Blitz for about a minute-and-a-half, then pour into a tall glass.

Smash the Maltesers to smithereens (all children love this bit!) and pour them into the glass. Give it a stir with a swizzle stick or long spoon and top with the mini marshmallows.

Makes one sinful glass

Perfect for sleepovers, parties or days with a 'Y'

family fuel

Simple, healthy recipes that are easy to make and perfect for children to lend a hand with should they feel like it. For when you do find yourself with more time, I've also included some recipes that can't be described as in any way grand, but which do take a bit longer. This is when you should enlist the children's help – they always seem to eat more when they've had a hand in the preparation

chilli chocolate wraps

Don't baulk at the idea of these for kids. While the chilli kicks,

it's not overpowering and the novelty value of the cocoa powder

appeals to most children's sense of the ridiculous and adds depth

1 tablespoon of olive oil

2 onions, finely chopped

3 fat cloves of garlic, finely chopped

450g (14 $^1/_2$ oz) of best minced beef

1 teaspoon of crushed cumin seeds

2 400g tins of plum tomatoes

2 tablespoons of sun-dried
   tomato paste

1 teaspoon of chilli powder

1 teaspoon of cocoa powder
   (I prefer Green & Black's)

Freshly ground black pepper and salt

8 soft tortillas

50g (1 $^1/_2$ oz) of Parmesan, grated

Small tub of soured cream

Handful of fresh coriander leaves

1 fresh lime

On the simmering plate, heat the olive oil in a large oven-proof pan or casserole with a lid. Fry the onions and garlic. Add the mince; fry until brown. Add the cumin seeds. Pour in the tomatoes and chop them in the pan. Add the tomato paste, chilli and cocoa powder and stir. Add salt and pepper and cover the pan. Transfer it to the simmering oven for 1-2 hours. Wrap the tortillas in foil and heat in the roasting oven for about 5 minutes. Place two good tablespoons of the chilli mix in each tortilla, then add some Parmesan, a good dollop of soured cream and fresh coriander leaves. Roll the tortillas and serve with lime wedges.

Serves 2

pizza-topped baked potatoes

My children are pizza obsessed – they love the lovely stringy Mozzarella. They also like baked potatoes, so this is the perfect combination. You can add extra toppings, but I prefer them like this

2 large potatoes
3 large ripe vine tomatoes
Teaspoon of olive oil
$1/2$ teaspoon of sun-dried tomato purée
Sprinkling of dried oregano
Tiny pinch of salt
Freshly ground black pepper
1 Mozzarella cheese

Cut the potatoes in half and put them on a rack in a roasting tin and bake in the roasting oven, with the grid shelf on the bottom set of runners, for around 45 minutes, depending on the size. Pop the tomatoes in a bowl of boiling water for a couple of minutes. Take the bowl to the sink and leave it under the running tap until the tomatoes have cooled. Peel the skins with a sharp knife, then blitz them in a blender. In a bowl, mix together the tomatoes, olive oil, tomato purée, oregano, salt and pepper. When the potatoes are done, take them out of the Aga and spread the tomato mixture on them. Slice the Mozzarella and place on the top. Pop the roasting tin back in the Aga, as high as it will go, and leave for about 5 minutes. Check the cheese has browned and is bubbly; if not, pop them back in for another couple of minutes. Serve with salad, or as my children prefer, Heinz Spaghetti!

Serves 4

Two favourites in one. What could be better?

robbie's sausage surprise

This recipe was created by Robbie, the son of a friend, for a
Year 9 pasta project. It's perfect for children to cook and is
a fantastic weekday supper that's also ridiculously easy to make

4 thick pork sausages
200g (8 oz) of coloured pasta
1 tablespoon of vegetable oil
1 red pepper, sliced
1 onion, sliced
100g (4 oz) of mushrooms, sliced
200g (8 oz) tin of sweetcorn
400g (16 oz) tin of chopped tomatoes
Pinch of dried mixed herbs
Salt and pepper
100g (4 oz) of Mozzarella, sliced

Place the sausages on the rack of the small Aga roasting tin and hang on the top set of runners in the roasting oven and cook until done. Cook the pasta in boiling, salted water for 10 minutes, or according to the instructions on the packet. Drain well and set aside. Fry the onion and pepper in oil in a large frying pan for about 5 minutes. Add the mushrooms and fry for 1 minute. Stir in the sweetcorn, tomatoes, herbs and seasoning. Slice each sausage into 8 and add to the pan. Place the cooked pasta in the pan and mix everything together. Put everything in an ovenproof dish and top with Mozzarella. Place on the grid shelf on the floor of the roasting oven for 5-10 minutes until the cheese has melted and started to brown. Serve with garlic bread.

Serves 4

If only all school work tasted so good!

individual toad-in-the-hole

Jack, who's seven, was absolutely enraptured the first time I made this for him. A big fan of sausages, his delight that something different could be done with them was palpable

Butter, for greasing
6 chipolatas
125g (4 $^1/_2$ oz) of plain flour
2 large eggs
150ml (5 fl oz) of milk
Muffin tray with six spaces

Lightly grease the muffin tray and place one chipolata in each hole. Cook on the floor of the roasting oven for 3 minutes.

Take it out and turn the chipolatas over. Then put it back in for another couple of minutes.

While it's cooking, put the flour into a bowl, make a well in the middle and stir in the eggs. Gradually add the milk, until you have a smooth batter. Add the salt and pepper. Alternatively, you can simply throw everything into a mixer and whiz for a few minutes.

Take the muffin tray out of the Aga, pour the batter over the sausages and put back in the roasting oven, on the third set of runners, for about 15 minutes.

Serve with salad, broccoli and cauliflower – or Heinz Baked Beans!

Makes 6

fish fingers and aga oven chips

If, like me, you were a child of the 70s, this was the very best supper to fill you up ready to play on your Spacehopper. And because these are home made, they won't be the same lurid orange!

2 smallish haddock fillets
125g (4 $1/2$ oz) of self-raising flour
150ml (5 fl oz) of lager
   (organic if possible)
Salt and black pepper
6 potatoes
Sunflower oil

Cut the potatoes into chips. Cover in a little sunflower oil and place on a baking tray on the floor of the roasting oven for about 30-40 minutes, turning them occasionally to make sure they cook evenly.

Cut the haddock into strips. Set aside a couple of spoonfuls of flour. Mix the rest of the flour, the lager and the salt and pepper together in a mixer.

The batter should be thick and gloopy – if it feels too thin, add some more flour. Dip the haddock strips in the flour and then the batter.

In a large frying pan, heat about 1cm (half an inch) of oil until it's smoking. Add the fish to the pan and cook for a few minutes until the batter turns golden. Carefully lift out the fish and place it on a baking sheet (hard-anodised if possible).

Put the baking sheet on the grid shelf on the third set of runners in the roasting oven and cook for a further 5 minutes or so.

Serves 2

parmesan-coated chicken strips

These are such a good alternative to frozen chicken nuggets and they only take a few minutes longer. The coating can also be used on whole chicken breasts for a fab chicken sandwich

2 skinned, boneless chicken breasts
1 egg
2 tablespoons of Parmesan
3 tablespoons of breadcrumbs
Pinch of cayenne or black pepper

I like to use organic, corn-fed chicken for this recipe as I think the succulent flavour of the chicken works well with the slightly crunchy coating.

My boys are great fans of turkey dinosaurs – regarding them as the height of culinary indulgence – so I occasionally use this coating for turkey escallops, though I suspect they would still prefer them in the shape of a T-Rex!

Cut the chicken into strips, then break the egg into a small bowl and whisk a little. Brush the chicken with the egg. Mix together the Parmesan, breadcrumbs and pepper. Dip the chicken in the mixture.

Place the chicken on a baking sheet, lined with Bake-O-Glide and put it on the floor of the roasting oven. Cook for about 15 minutes, turning the chicken over halfway through.

Children love these best with a pile of home-made Aga oven chips (see page 32 for the recipe).

Serves 2

creamy carbonara

Purists might turn their noses up at cream in a carbonara,

but I think it gives it wonderful depth and the children adore it

1 packet of bacon (about 6 rashers)
1 tablespoon of olive oil
6 tablespoons of white wine
1 packet of fresh spaghetti
6 egg yolks
6 tablespoons of double cream
40g (1 $^1/_2$ oz) of freshly grated Parmesan
Black pepper
1 tablespoon of butter

Put a huge pan of water, with lots of salt, on to the boiling plate. Cut the bacon into smallish pieces and fry slowly in a large pan on the simmering plate, with the olive oil and a little butter. When the bacon starts to get crispy, add the wine to the pan and let it cook for a few minutes. Remove the pan from the heat and set it aside until everything else is ready.

Once the water has boiled, add the pasta and cook according to the instructions. Mix together the egg yolks, cream, Parmesan and black pepper.

When the pasta is ready, put the bacon back on the simmering plate and drain the spaghetti. Turn the spaghetti into the pan with the bacon. Oosh it around a bit and then remove from the heat. Add the eggy, cheesy mix and allow it to stand either on top of the simmering plate lid or close to the Aga.

Take your time – the gentle heat will ensure a beautifully creamy sauce and will mean you won't end up with a mix that's altogether too firm.

Serves 4 (or 2 in our house)

perfect fish supper

This is so reminiscent of my own childhood suppers that I often eat it if I'm feeling miserable or am battling a deadline. The children love it as it's both comforting and easy to eat when they're tired

4 large potatoes
Tablespoon of olive oil
Butter
2 thick pieces of haddock
Maldon salt
Freshly ground black pepper
4 tablespoons of double cream

Boil a pan of water on the boiling plate. Peel the potatoes (and cut in half if you think they may be too large). Drop them into the water and cook until tender.

While this is going on, heat the olive oil in a cast-iron frying pan on the simmering plate. Then add a tablespoon of butter. When it starts to bubble, carefully place the fish in the pan and leave it for a minute or two. Delicately turn over the fish and do the same on the other side. Sprinkle over the salt and black pepper and transfer the pan to the roasting oven.

The grid shelf should be on the floor; place the pan on to it. Leave it there for 6-8 minutes, checking it doesn't get overdone.

Drain the potatoes and mash them. Beat in a tablespoon of butter and the cream, adding a pinch of salt and the black pepper as you go.

Serve with lots of freshly buttered bread.

Serves 2

I cook this dish when I'm feeling a bit grumpy

…or the whole world seems to be against me!

tarragon chicken

Few children dislike roast chicken and, though it takes a while to cook, there's nothing complicated in the preparation. I often cook this when the children have friends round after school. It's absolutely scrumptious served with tons of roast potatoes

1 chicken, organic, corn-fed
2 cloves of garlic
Small bunch of tarragon, chopped
Maldon salt
Butter

Chop the garlic into small pieces. Make some small incisions in the chicken breasts and thighs and push a small bit of garlic and tarragon under the skin.

Smear the chicken with butter and sprinkle the salt all over. Stand the chicken on a grill rack in the full-size roasting tin. Make a dome out of silver foil and put it over the chicken.

Slide the tin into the roasting oven on the lowest set of runners. Cook for 20 minutes per 500g (18 oz) plus 30 minutes.

Take the foil off about 45 minutes before the end of the cooking time to allow the chicken to brown.

Serve with mashed or roast potatoes, rice or a crisp green salad.

Serves 4

Although this does take a little time to prepare

meatballs with spaghetti

When the children have overdosed on PlayStation or are becoming naughty, I often drag them into the kitchen to make this

For the meatballs

250g (9 oz) of minced pork

250g (9 oz) of minced beef

1 egg

3 tablespoons of grated Parmesan

2 garlic cloves

1 tablespoon of chives, chopped

1 tablespoon of basil, chopped

4 tablespoons of breadcrumbs

Salt and black pepper

For the sauce

1 tablespoon of olive oil

1 onion, finely chopped

4 garlic cloves, chopped

Handful of basil, shredded

2 400g tins (14 fl oz) of organic tomatoes

150ml (5 fl oz) of water

Salt and freshly ground pepper

100ml (4 fl oz) of single cream

For the meatballs

Put all the ingredients into a bowl and mix together with a wooden spoon. Once everything is combined, shape the mixture into balls.

For the sauce

Heat the olive oil in a large pan on the simmering plate. Add the onion and gently cook for about five minutes. Add the garlic and half the basil and cook for another couple of minutes. Add the tomatoes and the water with the seasoning. Cook for about 10 minutes. Add the cream and stir, then the meatballs. Transfer to the simmering oven for about an hour, adding the last of the basil in the last few minutes. Serve the meatballs on top of large plates of steaming spaghetti.

Serves 6

it's well worth it – pure childhood comfort food

comforting risotto

With an Aga, a risotto needs little attention as it spends most of its time in the simmering oven. It's impossibly comforting and, as many babies' first spoonful of food is rice, it's a taste most children adore

Tablespoon of butter
2 chicken breasts, diced
1 onion, finely chopped
320g (11$^1/_2$ oz) of Arborio rice
1 glass of dry white wine (optional)
1 litre (1$^3/_4$ pints) of hot chicken or
   vegetable stock
$^1/_2$ tablespoon of butter
Freshly grated Parmesan

In a heavy bottomed oven-proof pan sauté the onion, chicken and bacon in the butter. Cook on the simmering plate for about 5 minutes.

Add the rice and mix well until it's coated and cook until it's utterly transparent. Add the wine if you want to and stir until it's evaporated or has been absorbed. Move the pan to the boiling plate, add the stock and bring to the boil. Transfer it to the floor of the simmering oven and leave for around 20 minutes.

Check all the liquid has been absorbed and that the rice is tender and creamy, but still firm to the bite.

Stir in the butter and Parmesan and serve with salad.

Serves 4

kitchen capers

It's important children spend time in the kitchen having fun. It shouldn't matter how good the results are – it's all in the journey. Cooking with children is one of life's purest pleasures. Who wouldn't get excited at the thought of licking gooey cake mixture off a spoon or cleaning out the mixing bowl! Most of these recipes involve baking because, frankly, that's what children like best…

Time to put on the aprons, hand out the wooden

best-ever chocolate cake

Moist, slightly gooey, with big chunks of chocolate, this is delicious served warm with ice cream. But it's also perfect for lunchboxes or after-school tea. Let the fun begin!

250g (8 oz) of softened butter
250g (8 oz) of golden caster sugar
4 eggs
Teaspoon of vanilla extract
3 tablespoons of Green & Black's
  cocoa powder
4 tablespoons of full-fat milk
250g (8 oz) of self-raising flour
100g (4 $^1/_2$ oz) bar of best milk chocolate
  (I use Lindt)

Beat together the butter and sugar. Add the egg and vanilla extract. Mix in the cocoa powder and milk. Slowly add the flour, beating all the time to ensure the mixture doesn't get lumpy. Smash the chocolate to pieces (children adore doing this bit) or, alternatively, throw everything into an electric mixer and whiz for a few minutes.

Pour the cake mixture into a round greased tin. For a three- or four-oven Aga, place the cake tin on the grid shelf on the floor of the baking oven and cook for about 20-25 minutes.

For a two-oven Aga, place the cake tin on the grid shelf on the floor of the roasting oven and place the plain shelf on the second set of runners. Bake for about 20-25 minutes. Test with a knife or skewer.

Serves 4

spoons and have some serious cooking fun!

spongy pear tart

My children adore this topsy-turvy recipe. It goes in one way and comes out the other. Much debate centres on the pattern the pears should make, but that's soon forgotten as it comes out of the Aga

Tablespoon of butter

Tablespoon of golden syrup

Small tin of pears in syrup

125g (4 oz) of softened, unsalted butter

125g (4 oz) of caster sugar

2 eggs

125g (4 oz) of self-raising flour

Half a teaspoon of vanilla extract

Grease a small, round cake tin with the butter. Pour in the golden syrup and mix around a bit. Drain and slice the pears (keeping back a tablespoon of their syrup for later) and arrange at the bottom of the tin.

Beat together the butter and sugar. Add the egg, the vanilla extract and the pear syrup. Slowly add the flour, beating all the time to ensure the mixture doesn't get lumpy. Alternatively, you can throw everything into an electric mixer and whiz it for a few minutes.

Pour the cake mixture over the pears.

For a three- or four-oven Aga, place the cake tin on the grid shelf on the floor of the baking oven and cook for 20-25 minutes.

For a two-oven Aga, place cake tin on the grid shelf on the floor of the roasting oven and place the plain shelf on the second set of runners. Bake for about 20-25 minutes, then test with a knife or skewer. Serve warm with cream or ice cream.

Serves 6-8

fairy cakes

Every child should bake at least one batch of fairy cakes. The sheer joy of licking the cake mixture from the spoon or dying the icing a lurid shade is a quintessentially childish pleasure

For the cakes

125g (4 oz) of softened unsalted butter
125g (4 oz) of caster sugar
Half a teaspoon of vanilla extract
2 eggs
125g (4 oz) of self-raising flour

The easiest way to make fairy cakes is to throw everything into a food processor, but much of the fun for children is in the mixing. So, with wooden spoon at the ready here's what to do…

Cream together the butter and sugar, add the vanilla extract and then the eggs. When the mixture has come together, start to add the flour a little at a time, beating until you've used it all. Spoon the mixture into paper cases lining a muffin tray.

For a three- or four-oven Aga, place the muffin tray on the grid shelf on the floor of the baking oven and cook for about 15-20 minutes.

For a two-oven Aga, place the muffin tray on the grid shelf on the floor of the roasting oven and place the plain shelf on the second set of runners. Bake for 10-12 minutes.

Makes about 12

See over for decorating tips

No one should reach their teenage years without

having made a batch of colourful fairy cakes…

Tissue paper-lined boxes decorated by children

decorating your fairy cakes

Here's where your child should be allowed to indulge in utter artistic freedom. A fairy cake decorated by oneself tastes infinitely nicer when you're small and parents should not try to dictate the pattern!

For the glacé icing

225g (8 oz) of icing sugar

2-4 tablespoons of hot water

Food colouring (optional)

Sift the icing sugar into a bowl. Slowly add enough water to give you a smooth icing that is thick enough to coat the back of a spoon. Add extra water if it is too thick or extra sugar if it becomes a little runny.

When it comes to food colouring, less is definitely more. If you don't want all the cakes to be iced in the same colour then remove a small amount of the icing to another bowl and add the smallest drip of colouring. You can always add more until you achieve the desired shade.

Some decorating tips

Plain white icing looks fab when topped by a single crystallised rose or violet petal.

Rice paper flowers are a nostalgia-trip for anyone who's reached 30 and are so pretty. Children can plonk one on a cake and feel they've created a work of art.

Dolly mixtures look and taste yummy and single colour dolly mixture fairy cakes have, to a-five-year-old, an indefinable sophistication.

Writing icing now comes in handy little tubes, perfect for small hands, and in a wide array of colours. Older children can write messages, while smaller children can create their own patterns.

and containing lovingly made cakes are fab gifts

This dough makes a quite perfect pizza base…

our daily bread

Freshly baked bread is heavenly and startlingly easy to make.

I can't understand why any Aga owner would want a bread maker

when the Aga is the ultimate bread making machine

650g (1lb 7 $^1/_2$ oz) of strong white
   bread flour
1 teaspoon of salt
$^1/_2$ teaspoon of sugar
1 sachet of instant dried yeast
Good splash of olive oil
400ml (14 fl oz) of warm water
   (1 part boiling, 2 parts cold)

Mix the dry ingredients together, add the olive oil and stir. Slowly start to add the water and mix until it becomes a dough.

Turn out on to a lightly floured surface and knead for about 10 minutes. You can use an electric mixer with a dough hook if you like, but there is something so wonderfully earthy about kneading it by hand that it would seem a shame. Put the dough back into the bowl and cover it with a clean tea towel. Then it needs to go somewhere warm. A surface next to the Aga is perfect. Leave for about an hour or until the dough has doubled in size.

Uncover and shape the dough into a loaf and put on a piece of Bake-O-Glide in a loaf tin or on a baking tray. Put it back in the warm place and leave for another 30 minutes. Then bake in the roasting oven, with the grid shelf on the floor, for about 20 minutes or until the bread is golden and sounds hollow when tapped.

Makes a standard white loaf

Also, try dough balls with pasta dishes or salad

mini pizzas

Making your own supper is such fun when you're small. Pizzas are perfect – they encourage a love of cooking while also allowing for boundless artistic enthusiasm. Get set for a mini adventure…

Pizza dough (see recipe on page 57)
400g (14 oz) tin of tomatoes
1 tablespoon of tomato purée
Olive oil
Salt and pepper
Two Mozzarella cheeses, sliced
Fresh basil leaves

Divide the dough into equal pieces. You can make any size pizzas you like. If you have too much dough, then bake some dough balls or garlic bread to go with your supper or some rolls for tomorrow's lunchboxes.

Set the pizza dough, evenly spaced, on greased baking sheets.

Open the tin of tomatoes and drain the juice. Blitz the tomatoes in a processor and add the purée, olive oil, salt and pepper. Blend gently. Spoon the tomato mixture over the pizza bases, distributing it evenly. Leave a gap around the edges so you'll get an uncovered crust.

Pop on the sliced Mozzarella and top with anything else you fancy – ham, mushrooms, sweetcorn, tuna, bacon, pepperoni, the list goes on.

Pop the baking sheet on to the floor of the roasting oven and bake for between 10 and 20 minutes, depending on the size of the pizza.

Drawn by Jack James
age 7

"With children, all you can do is make cooking

and eating as much fun as it can be…"

details

Fish
FishWorks Direct delivers more than 24 types of fish, 10 varieties of shellfish and five smoked seafoods direct to the door. Call on 0800 0523717 or visit www.fishworks.co.uk

Meat
Donald Russell Direct offers truly wonderful meat which is vacuum packed so it lasts longer in the fridge. Call 01467 629666 or visit the website at www.donaldrussell.com

Eggs
I can't stress enough the importance of using free-range organic eggs. For Freedom Farm Eggs, call Farmaround on 020 7627 8066.

Cheese
Neals Yard Dairy on 020 7240 5700 is one of the best places to get an extensive range of cheeses.

Cookware
There are Aga Shops throughout the UK stocking a comprehensive range of cookware. Call 08457 125207 to be directed to your nearest store. The shops also host regular cookery demonstrations and events.

Aga Magazine
A quarterly title with a 16-page recipe section in every issue. To subscribe, call 01562 734040.

Agalinks
Agalinks has a huge database of recipes from a host of chefs and cookery writers, including Mary Berry and Louise Walker. It's also home to the Aga Cookery Doctor, who will answer culinary questions and offer hints for successful cooking. Visit www.agalinks.com

Useful information no cook should be without...

thanks

As ever, there are so many to thank…

Firstly, my gorgeous children – Lucie, Tatti, Jack and Toby – who's energy and enthusiasm are all-inspiring.

Secondly, my friends who've helped by providing advice and ideas. They include Patty, Maggie, Linda, Jayne and Pauline.

My fabulous publisher, Jon Croft, is owed a huge debt of gratitude, as are Matt and Meg at Absolute Press, for putting up with both my lateness and my somewhat demanding nature!

I'd like also to thank Steve Jellings, Phil Beckett and Adrian Thorn (they'll know why!).

Enormous thanks to Andy and Penny for being picture perfect.

And finally my thanks to Tim, who has entered into the spirit of this book with gusto – there's something utterly sweet about seeing a grown man tucking enthusiastically into a dainty, Barbie-pink fairy cake!

Laura
Norfolk, Autumn 2003

"Mummy, when are we going to stop writing about all this food and start eating it?"